Narcissistic Mothers

Healing guide on how to handle manipulative parents and other abuses, fix the relationship

Caroline Anderson

Introduction

Narcissistic mothers are exhausting. If you have one or have ever had one, you know that walking on eggshells is more than an idiom—it's a way of life. Narcissistic mothers make most people around them (family members, friends, and even therapists) feel crazy. Why is it that no matter what you do or say, they always find a way to fault you? And they do it in such a way that makes you second-guess yourself. They are master manipulators who make the "blame game" their favorite sport. But what if these same exact behaviors could be explained by the fact that your mother is a narcissistic personality?

Living with these people can be soul-wrenching because they lack empathy and feed off of the energy of others around them. Their destructive habits can turn every relationship into a mine-field of emotional land mines waiting to go off at any moment. But it doesn't have to be this way.

You can change it, and it is completely in your hands. In this book, we are going to deal with the various problems associated with being raised by a narcissistic mother, how it affects your personality, and how you can get out of this toxic environment. I agree that the process might not be easy, and it will take a lot of work. But the most important thing to remember is that healing is not impossible. It takes a lot of courage, patience, and practice. But if you have the right guidance and tools, you can practice healthy habits and develop clear boundaries with your narcissistic mother.

I also understand that as a daughter, it is not easy for you to view your mother as a source of negativity in your life, but you also have to understand that it is what it is. Giving in to the blind love for your mother even if she has a toxic nature would only leave you with trauma and a distorted personality.

The Narcissistic Personality

Traits Overt vs. Covert narcissistic personality disorder traits Overt refers to apparent features. On the other hand, covert refers to the set of hidden attributes and not openly displayed.

Overt Traits

- Always wants to be at the center of attention

- Monopolize conversation

- Exaggerate their achievements

- React with impatience and anger when the accomplishments of others disagree

- Criticize often

- Display arrogance to those they deem inferior

- Have anger issues and often result in violence

- Display unhealthy competition

- Expect exceptional treatment for no good reason

- Always shift blame

Covert Traits

- Emotional manipulation to get their way

- Insensitive and often withhold affection

- Seek out empathic people to exploit

- Often complain of victimization

- Stage-manage crisis (or at least exaggerate) for attention

- Comes across as emotionally needy

These overt and covert traits are two sides of the same coin. If you notice either set of these signs, the other is in there somewhere. It is just a matter of time, and it will rear its face.

Pathological Aspects of Narcissism

These are the aspects that are brought about by the distortion of the brain due to the disorder. They include:

- A heightened sense of self-importance

- A deep need for attention

- Lack of empathy

- Envy

- Inflated sense of entitlement

- Great fantasies of success

- Need for control

- Fragile self-esteem

Invisible Traits of Narcissism

These refer to that part of the narcissist that is concealed by the appearance of confidence. Beneath the surface, things are not as steady as they seem.

Narcissists tend to be:

- Highly vulnerable to criticism

- Prone to anxiety and depression

- Unstable self-esteem

- Obsessed with their self-image

- Have difficulty in relationships insecure

- Difficulty in regulating emotions

This instability makes them always seek others to keep them inflated.

There you have it. Now you can easily be able to identify a narcissist.

What is NPD?

Narcissistic Personality Disorder (NPD) is characterized by a long-term pattern of abnormal self-views, abnormal perceptions of others, and often, distorted self-worth and interpersonal relationships. But it is also one of the most difficult disorders to spot and articulate because its victims are usually intelligent and able to function at a high level. Victims are brought into therapy by concerned family members who innocently wonder why their nearest or dearest seem so distant or cold (a "cold" narcissist). The narcissist's rage at being discovered is immense because he feels his deception has been unearthed. The narcissist, in fact, is the devious one. He is adept at feigning emotions, misled by the conviction that he can convincingly pretend to be "normal" and thereby deflect accurate diagnosis.

The DSM-IV-TR distinguishes two subtypepes of NPD: arrogant and vulnerable. The vulnerable narcissist is described as diffusely preoccupied with thoughts and feelings of inadequacy, shame, and low self-worth. He often feels sad and lonely. He usually presents himself as a victim and seeks constant but perceived affirmation from others. As opposed to the classic NPD, he is rarely confrontational or arrogant.

The DSM-IV-TR also distinguishes between high-functioning or "compensatory" narcissists (HNCs) and "grandiose" or "malignant" ones (GNCs). HNCs appear to be secure, upbeat, self-assured, outgoing, and pleasant.

Types of Narcissistic Mothers

Narcissism has become such a now and again utilized word in a traditional culture that it has taken on its very own existence. It's being used for everything extending from an approach to casually affront somebody to a method for talking about unscripted television stars' conduct. The word has even been applied unpredictably to depict whole social ages.

Even though it might have an informal definition that isn't leaving at any point soon, the expression "narcissist" still has a quite specific indicative description in the psychological well-being field. The term is applied to somebody who meets the criteria for determining Narcissistic Personality Disorder (NPD), which are spread out in the Diagnostic and Statistical Manual of Mental Disorders, Fifth Edition.

People who meet the criteria for having NPD can be commonly portrayed as having a conviction of prevalence over others that gives them the privilege of special treatment and a fixation on self-important dreams of accomplishment and power. Where it counts, be that as it may, they are truly powerless against analysis and sentiments of disgrace and try hard to ensure their delicate consciences. They are likewise self-assimilated and have lower levels of compassion for other people. This may lead them to exploit individuals as they continued looking for over the top consideration and appreciation.

Narcissism exists along with a range, be that as it may, and each individual who is determined to have NPD doesn't hold fast flawlessly to this portrayal. Specialists have recognized three significant sorts of narcissists, each with its very own blend of characteristics. Every one of the three classes has various techniques for ensuring the delicate internal center feeling of self, and one of them may even have an alternate inspiration. Inside every one of the three sorts, additional sub-types describe how the characteristics may appear to other people.

These various kinds and sub-types are examined by a wide range of scientists and emotional wellness experts.

Notwithstanding, they regularly utilize different marks to portray the equivalent "type." moreover, in some cases, the analysts use a similar name for two unique classifications in any event when they are depicting the same sort or sub-type. This makes comprehension of the types of narcissists exceptionally hard to get a handle on.

Three Major Narcissist Types

The Malignant Type

Otherwise called Toxic Narcissists, they are exceptionally manipulative and exploitative. These narcissists have numerous solitary qualities absent in the other two significant sorts and are regularly contrasted and sociopaths and mental cases. They frequently have a perverted streak that makes them not the same as the different two significant sorts. Their essential objective is to command and control, and they will utilize double-dealing and hostility to achieve it and need regret for their activities. They may even appreciate the suffering of others.

The Vulnerable Type

Otherwise called Fragile, Compensatory or Closet Narcissists, regardless of whether they are better than a great many people they meet, they disdain the spotlight in any case. They regularly try to append themselves to uncommon individuals as opposed to looking for exceptional treatment themselves. They may look for pity or charm others through excessive liberality to get the consideration and profound respect they have to help their self-esteem.

The Classic Type

These are the consideration looking for narcissists who boast about their achievements, anticipate that others should complement them, and feel qualified for special treatment. They get exhausted when the focal point of the discussion goes to anybody yet themselves, and once in a while, they prefer to impart the spotlight to other people. The contradiction is that they are frantic to feel significant. Simultaneously, they regularly see themselves to be better than a great many people with whom they come into contact.

Sub-Types

Covert Vs. Overt

This sub-type depicts whether the narcissist utilizes techniques to get their needs met progressively out in the open or whether those strategies are increasingly stealthy and hidden. For instance, both covert and overt narcissists may put individuals down, brag, and search for chances to exploit individuals; however, overt narcissists do as such indefinite and perceptible.

Manners. Covert narcissists work off the camera or are progressively uninvolved forceful. Others may leave away, not realizing they were controlled, or the narcissist's strategies may enable the person in question to deny what occurred.

Cerebral Vs. Somatic

This sub-type characterizes what the narcissist values in oneself and others. Neither one of the subs types needs to be eclipsed by their accomplice. However, they do need somebody around who upgrades their status because, to them, their accomplices are objects they can flaunt as though to state, "Look what I just acquired for my gathering."

Somatic narcissists are fixated on their bodies, youth, and outer appearance, investing a great deal of energy at the exercise center and before mirrors.

Cerebral narcissists are simply the smarty pants and consider themselves the most astute ones in the room, attempting to intrigue individuals with their achievements and places of intensity. Any of the three sorts of narcissists, malignant, vulnerable, or classic, can be both of these two sub-types.

Inverted

A few analysts have distinguished an uncommon sort of secretive, defenseless narcissist called a rearranged narcissist. These narcissists are believed to be mutually dependent. They try to connect themselves to different narcissists to feel unique and possibly fulfilled or cheerful when involved with other narcissists. They are unfortunate casualty narcissists who experience the ill effects of youth surrender issues.

Since the term narcissist is utilized so much of the time and in such a self-assertive way, it has turned out to be hard to tell when it ought to be paid attention to, or even to what gathering of individuals the term is being applied. Albeit all narcissists can conceivably be exploitative, not all narcissists are similar, and one of them is hazardous. Malignant narcissists can be dangerous and injurious. Because they try to command others, do not have a still, small voice, and appreciate the harm they cause, communications with them will probably be destructive.

Figuring out how to recognize these sorts and comprehend which type is being examined in perusing material about narcissism is essential.

If you are being abused, misused, or mishandled by anybody, in any case, it doesn't make a difference what sort of narcissist they are or regardless of whether they're a narcissist by any stretch of the imagination.

How Narcissism Manifests Itself in Your Mother?

The society we live in is one that values collectivism and holds it in quite a high regard. This automatically means that we have been conditioned to put other people's feelings and emotions before our own, even more so when these people are our close ones, be it friends or family. Such an outlook towards relationships and feelings leads to the passing on burden and trauma from one generation to the other. This is even more applicable within women, as they are expected to act in a more emotionally mature way, taking charge of solving interpersonal conflicts, particularly within the confines of their home. However, a lot of these conflicts generate from reasons beyond their control; they are reflections of taxing and complicated patterns of action and behavior on the part of other people, and not being mindful enough of these patterns further increases the emotional complexity women need to encounter on a fairly regular basis. Speaking about the origin of these patterns, the immediate focus needs to be turned not to the women, but to their parents, and more importantly, their mothers, whom they have in all likelihood idolized and looked up to for the majority of their lives, without recognizing the possible pitfalls a daughter has to suffer in the face of bad parenting.

Children- especially daughters- bear the mark of their mothers' problematic behaviors for ages, even a lifetime, and often there are no healthy ways to redress this because they are not able to identify the root cause of such behavior. In our society, we are brought up in a way that we have been constantly taught and reminded how our parents are perfect, how they are absolutely incapable of making any mistakes, which is exactly why we find it very hard to even acknowledge where they have gone wrong- both as individuals and as parents and caregivers. Acknowledging and identifying their mother's problematic behavior is the very first step daughters can take in order to redress the neglect and/or abuse they have faced, followed by looking at such behavioral patterns in closer detail to unveil the tiny ways of microaggressions in which they have been treated by their mothers. Treating faulty parental behavior analytically, in a step-by-step manner, is perhaps the best way for anyone to shift the responsibility and blame for a lot that has gone wrong in the past from themselves to their parents, whose behavior has actually accelerated the process directly or indirectly. In this chapter, we would be concentrating on narcissism and how it manifests in mothers. The chapter is broken into two larger sections. The first one looks at the behavior of narcissistic mothers, and the second one highlights how these behavioral patterns can very easily turn into abuse and how to recognize those forms of abuse coming from a parent.

Behavior of a Narcissistic Mother

Narcissistic personality disorder (or NPD) is an axis I mental disorder as categorized in the DSM (the Diagnostic and Statistical Manual for Mental Disorders), and like any other disorders, NPD can also range between mild, moderate, and severe- all causing considerable distress to both the person affected as well as the people around them. Caregiving for people suffering from narcissistic disorder is really difficult as they themselves are, most of the time completely oblivious of the fact that they are going through some sort of mental distress. Such dynamics, therefore, become even trickier in the parent-daughter relationship because a lot of implicit caregiving is already expected by a mother from their child.

Famous educator and psychologist Nina W. Brown (2001), in her book *Children of the Self-Absorbed: A Grown Up's Guide to Getting over Narcissistic Parents*, mentions how many mothers display what can be clinically termed as a "destructive narcissistic pattern." The signs of a destructive narcissistic parent, or DNP, are reflected in the mother's attitude, action, and expectations from their children, which are primarily guided by the mother's need to have the reversal of a mother-daughter relationship. This way, the mother would invariably be at the receiving end of their child's care and attention and would also be able to shrug off any potential responsibility that can come their way. Such a formulation is the result of a narcissistic mother's inner want (or need) of carefully preserving an image of themselves that is superior when compared to their daughters' and is perfect and entitled.

Some of the most easily noticeable signs of the behavior of a narcissistic mother can be (but are in no way limited to) have been briefly listed below.

<u>High Expectations of Caregiving</u>

Making their daughter solely responsible for their well-being and comfort is a classic sign of a controlling, manipulative, and narcissistic parent. Let us be real; it is very difficult, maybe even impossible, for a single person to be completely in charge of catering to all sorts of emotional needs for another person. This forms a very toxic and unhealthy bond between the mother and the daughter, which the mother thrives on because it feeds into their ego, while eating away at the limited energy the daughter has, all of which she needs to essentially direct towards her mother and nobody else, isolating herself from other important people in her life.

Excessive Criticism

Narcissistic mothers are constantly critical of anything and everything their daughters do, even when criticism is not welcome or needed. This form of criticism is also something that serves their own inflated sense of self-worth and is a constant reminder that other people (especially their daughters, whom they can directly control to a great extent) would never be as good as she is. However, they would not be willing to provide feedback or remedial measures for all the criticism they are handing out. In the guise of constructive criticism, they would try to make sure that they have shattered the confidence of their daughters, even if it is with regard to something their daughter is a lot more familiar with than they are.

High Standards and Expectations

They would always expect that everything is done in a way that would satisfy them, even if it is uncomfortable for the daughters. Narcissistic mothers always tend to put their needs before everyone else's and are blissfully oblivious about the discomfort they are causing to other people. Such parents also tend to create very high standards regarding any task they want their daughters to complete since that would ensure that they would be able to find more loopholes in how the task has been executed.

<u>Practicing Favoritism Among Their Children</u>

A result of bad parenting is to pick out favorites among one's own children. This can be even more visible in cases where there is a son and a daughter, out of which the son is preferred and usually showered affection on, but the daughter instead is held responsible for returning the same, even if they have been constantly neglected by their mothers. This specific controlling behavior has been expanded upon in the book *The Favorite Child: How a Favorite Impacts Every Family Member for Life* by Ellen Libby (2010). Any type of favoritism by such a parent is essentially targeted towards framing a 'golden child' and a 'scapegoat.' While the former is shaped in a way that the narcissist mother can see the perfection she holds so dearly to herself in them, the latter is the one left to do the clean-up, both for the mother as well as for the favorite child. The golden child simply becomes an extension of the self- centeredness of a narcissistic mother. It is wrong to say that the ones who are picked as favorites do not suffer in any way emotionally, but what they go through is monumentally less- in degree and in nature- when compared to the one who is not the favorite, the obvious receiver of the mother's love and attention.

Deliberately Not Communicating Their Needs

Requiring the daughter to be aware of their needs at all times without specifically listing them out, and getting offended if such unrealistically high standards of care are breached, is a tell-tale sign of a narcissistic mother. Nobody is a mind reader, and expecting other people to cater to someone's needs just by virtue of "if you know me well enough, you must know what I need at the moment" is a horrible way of treating anyone. This way, the daughter is not just easily susceptible to nitpicking and having their faults pointed out by the mother, but it is also ensured that well after an incident has passed, the daughter continued to feel guilt in retrospect because of the looming realization that they have failed to provide to their mother what she had provided for them for so many years.

Controlling Nature

One of the first ways in which a narcissistic mother would want to exert her dominance over their child's life is by trying to control them in many different ways, thus hinting that they are better at almost everything their daughters try to, humiliating their children on purpose in the process. This is a classic sign of manipulative behavior, which has been discussed in more detail later on in this chapter.

Persistent Need for the Spotlight

Such mothers would also attempt to divert all attention to their own self, which can go as far as to deliberately ruin special occasions for the daughter (and any other people involved) so that she becomes the center of attention even if the situation does not concern her all that much. Everything needs to be about her and her only; any modification of this is not accepted well and is often met with violent and destructive behavior as the reaction.

However, even if you check 'yes' without any second thoughts to all of the behaviors marked on this list being exhibited by your mother, the chances are that you would still not be a hundred percent sure if your mother is narcissistic or not, because as already mentioned earlier, children are constantly expected to look past the mistake of their parents, forever shouldering the obligation towards them without pointing out any error on their part. Besides this, it is also true that every human being is indeed capable of making mistakes, and since human behavior is extremely unpredictable, it is hard to draw a line between unintentional mistakes on someone's part and deliberate narcissism. It is especially difficult for daughters to draw such a line with their mothers because of the emotional bond that exists between them. A healthy distance would help them to identify narcissism, but it is one of the first signs of a problematic parent that they would hold their daughters responsible for so many things to such a great extent that they are never fully emotionally capable of maintaining a healthy emotional distance. This further leads to even more controlling behavior by a narcissistic mother.

Another really problematic behavior that a narcissistic mother is very likely to display is the constant attempts at impressing people around her but who are not immediately close to her. Since perfectionism (according to her own terms) is of utmost importance to a person like this, she will go out of her way to create an outward appearance which gives most other people the impression that she is socially very successful, is well in control of all facets of her life, and so on. Once this kind of bubble has been created, it would be a lot easier for her to make other people believe how grossly incompetent their daughter is, especially when compared to herself. This leads to- and is facilitated by- constant dismissals of the daughter's success, rejection of the ways in which she deems fit to live her own life, belittling and comparing her with others (in private and in front of other people as well), and so on. Once other people are under the impression that the mother is so successful that her daughter can never possibly live up to that, such a pattern of dismissive behavior would then simply be multiplied many times through how other people react to the daughter and her ways of life. Although the disapproval from other people might not be as direct as the ones coming from an overtly narcissistic mother, they can take the form of pity, unwarranted sympathy, and other expressions which together contribute to undermining the daughter, thus adding on to what her mother gets out to her in the very first place.

Abuse of a Narcissistic Mother

Here, abuse does not mean direct physical abuse. It goes without saying that abuse can come at you in different forms, one so different from the other that you would never think of clubbing themselves together, but manifestations of the same ill intent, nevertheless. The abuse inflicted by a narcissistic mother is most likely to be emotional and psychological. It would make their daughters feel inadequate about what they have managed to achieve in their lives, driven by the non-stop criticism from their mothers no matter what. This feeling of inadequacy will, in turn, make them yet more vulnerable to being ill-treated by their mothers because a lowered level of self-esteem naturally makes people think that others would know what is better for them. Dealing with a narcissistic mother is a vicious cycle of abuse. It can be difficult to process but even more complex to identify in the first place, but you can use some of the following pointers as a starting point to shed light on abusive tendencies.

She Loves You, But Only With Terms and Conditions Applied

Your mother is controlling, and the love she is willing to give you is conditional. Either you live by her rules and be the subject of limited affection, or you are closed from any affection from her side. Conditional love is the characteristic feature of any emotionally immature parent, writes Lindsay Gibson (2015) in her book *Adult Children of Emotionally Immature Parents: How to Heal from Distant, Rejecting, or Self-involved Parents.*

Conditional love is extremely problematic not just because of its momentary effect on you, but even more because receiving affection only in exchange for adhering to some things would subconsciously push you even further to change things about yourself so that at one point, you can feel like you are receiving unconditional love and approval from your mother. However, on the other hand, she would expect you to love her unconditionally at all costs and in every situation.

It is your responsibility to make sure that she never has to fulfill any conditions ever in order to be the recipient of your affection. She does the opposite to you only because "she cares so much for you" and "she knows the best," and you obviously do not know enough, so the best way out for you is to grant her all your care and affection, to the extent that you end up almost revering her. First of all, any sort of conditional love is, of course, problematic, but the expectation of unconditional love and regard without leaving room for any constructive dialogue is equally harmful.

She Has No Sense of Boundaries

A surefire way to exert control is to show a clear disregard of any sort of personal boundaries. Encroaching on the daughter's personal life, their personal relationships, and friendships, which they have formed and nurtured beyond the restrictions of their family, is one of the many manipulative and toxic strategies of a narcissistic mother. Boundaries do not exist for her because healthy boundaries deny her the constant approval she demands from her daughter, and that is not something she can make her peace with. Any attempt by the daughter to establish boundaries is most likely to be met with very reactionary and volatile actions, to the extent that the daughter feels that it is more peaceful to let her mother into all realism of her life than to go through such volatile actions from her. Tricking someone into compromising on their own peace of mind is a very toxic trait of a narcissistic person and is one they really hold on to.

She Is Quick to Play the Victim or the Martyr Card

The victim card is the go-to excuse for most narcissistic people. Playing the victim card in every scenario helps them out because they can get out of facing any consequences for their action without necessarily having the spotlight taken away from them. And if they are not the victim in a situation, they are the martyr; they are knowingly making sacrifices for their daughter. But at no point in time does she check with the daughter if these 'sacrifices' are actually needed or not, if they are welcomed by the daughter or if they even benefit her in any way. So, basically, these sacrifices are being made so that the narcissist mother can comfort their sense of self-worth (which is ridiculously high). These are also made because these can serve as constant reminders for the mother to guilt their daughters into doing things for them, especially if they do not want to. Such mothers are ignorant on purpose about the importance of consent in interpersonal relationships and reap basic human decency to their own benefits in order to maintain the perceived sense of grandiosity in their heads.

She Is Beyond All Apologies, But Nobody Else Is

While constantly demanding apologies- not just verbally, but also in action- over and over again from you, even in situations where you are not really to blame, a narcissistic mother will always maintain that she is beyond apologies. The rule of saying sorry simply does not apply to her because even if she makes a mistake, it should be overlooked owing to the mere fact that she is your mother. This abusive tendency can actually reflect in different ways. Reminding their daughters that since she gave birth to them and brought them up, which is why the daughters should always be grateful to them regardless of how many times they mess up, is a classic way narcissistic mothers tend to excuse themselves from any kind of blame.

Citing their age, 'generation gap,' and so on to garner sympathy is another way they tend to establish that apologies should not be expected from here because any and all of her mistakes are purely unintentional. However, how we can understand if this is actually intended or not is to check for reciprocity. If the mother demands apologies from you according to her own terms and cannot seem to let small things go without you profusely seeking her approval, then it is surely a sign of narcissistic abuse.

Everything Is Always Very Personal for Her

She also tends to take everything personally because, in her mind, she is the most important person to have possibly ever existed, and therefore, she should always be reminded of the same by the people in her life. While she makes sure that there is some sort of explanation for any mistake on her part or any hurt she caused her daughters to face, not even the tiniest slip coming from the daughter would be tolerated by her. Even if unrelated, a narcissistic mother would always make everything about themselves, take the present and perceived details very personally, ending up creating huge, unprecedented scenes out of the most trivial of subjects. However, this is also one way you can absolutely not play her own cards against her and remind her of what she did to you once she acts in the same way with you or with anyone else. She will make the rules, and she will most certainly make them in a way that would favor nobody but her.

She Displays Manipulative Behavior

It is one thing to expect you to do every little thing her way, but it is far more problematic and abusive when your mother begins to manipulate you in small, unidentifiable ways that add up to a much larger impact on your mind. Manipulation can come in various ways, starting from "I know what is better from you" to "You are really selfish of caring more for yourself than you do for me." The aim of manipulation is fixed- to make you feel incompetent and doubt yourself so that your guards are lowered, and she can have her way with you without much resistance from your side because she has already made you believe that she means well. Manipulation can start at a very young age when the daughter is, of course, not aware of the ways in which they are being controlled by their narcissistic mother, and since those are the most formative years of a child's life, they might grow up to act and think in ways which would specifically fuel the irrational needs of a narcissistic mother. Unlearning becomes even harder in cases like these, but obviously not impossible.

She Is Extremely Vindictive

One of the most abusive traits displayed by narcissistic mothers is that they are vengeful and vindictive. Just like no slippage by their daughters ever misses their eyes, they also make sure to get back at their daughters for each and every one of these slippages and even more, to 'settle the score' when there was no match, no competition between the mother and the daughter in the first place. In order to settle this score, she will go out of her way to cause harm to her daughters, examples of which might include running a smear campaign against her, spreading rumors and false gossip behind her back, and doing everything within her power to create a bad reputation for her daughter. The extent of control and manipulation exhibited by a narcissistic mother often goes beyond the private sphere- the more people from outside she manages to get engaged through her conniving schemes, the greater she can assert dominance over her daughter.

She Is Emotionally Volatile and Unpredictable

First of all, if a person is completely emotionally unpredictable, then chances are very high that they need some kind of professional help for emotional regulation. Apart from this, intentional unpredictable behavior can be a distinct sign of abuse. Patients suffering from Narcissistic Personality Disorder are extremely emotionally volatile. Their reactions to any normal thing can drastically swing between fragility, violence, and cold rage depending on the outcomes they wish to gain out of leveraging their way through the situation at hand. Mothers who especially display such symptoms are coming from a place of stunted emotional development, resulting in significantly low self-esteem, which results in them not being able to face criticism, and hence, flaring up in multiple ways while facing a crisis.

Even in such a case, emotionally unpredictable behavior for an extended period of time can be a sign of abuse, especially if and when the person with such a pattern of behavior is unwilling to admit the problem and/or seek medical help. A lot of times, her volatile behavior is also almost planned in a way that the daughter is left behind to pick up the pieces and make things right, which is an indirect way of shifting the responsibility to fix things to the daughter. This would be done especially in front of other people by a narcissistic person so that they can guarantee that the humiliation they are making their daughter face is also public, and hence is etched into the memory of more people.

What needs to be kept in mind while dealing with any sort of problematic parenting is that none of this is in any way the daughter's fault. She is not to blame even a bit. In fact, the blame should be residing with the parents who are making, even forcing, their own children to go through such a troublesome experience. But you can only start over afresh if you are open to understanding your past and taking charge of your present life. It is only natural that revisiting a lot of memories of not being treated how any child should be might bring back unwanted feelings and repressed hurt, but living in denial of how that hurt was caused in the very first place is not the best coping mechanism. While trying to understand what has happened to you in the past, you might question yourself if this is the knowledge that would actually help you- if this is something you are better off not knowing, in fact. But self-knowledge makes way for self-reflection, which also helps you to distance yourself from people who have caused you hurt and then evaluate their actions. Holding the right person responsible for the way they have made you feel is the best step towards living a mindful and positive life.

While this chapter tells you how to identify the behavior and abusive patterns of a narcissistic parent, it does not tell you much about how to deal with it and what to do with all the new information you have now acquired. Breaking the cycle of abuse and reacting positively to it can sound like an unattainable and rather far-fetched idea, but it is not impossible at all. Through positive reinforcements and by unlearning the problematic associations we have been taught to make all our lives, it is absolutely possible to unlearn the lasting effects of neglect and mistreatment suffered at the hands of a self-absorbed and narcissistic parent. These sections will be discussed in a lot more detail in the coming chapters of this book, which would hopefully be helpful to all of you in dealing with similar problems in your own lives.

Daughters and Mothers

In a perfect world, your mother is supposed to be the first person you fall in love with because she is essentially the one who ushers you into this world. She is the one who nurtures you, supports you, and helps you discover yourself, as well as navigate your way through life and living. She is the one who makes you feel comfortable and secure. You learn about everything you need to know through her. You long for her to hold you, touch you, smile with you, and be there always. She treats you and how empathetic she is with you, dictates what you feel and desire, and help you understand your place in the world and how much you matter and value.

The narcissistic mother is supremely incapable of empathy, and as a result, she completely wrecks the development of her child on a psychological level.

All she ever sees in the child is her reflection and nothing more. As a result, she has no sense of boundaries. She is blissfully unaware of the distinct separation between herself and those who call her mother. She does not realize that her children are different individuals, all unique in their way, and all very deserving of her love and affection. No matter how the signs and symptoms of narcissistic personality disorder vary, one thing that stays constant is that the narcissist is the worst in parenting.

I should clarify that the effects of having a narcissistic mother differ when it comes to sons and daughters. More often than not, the girls will spend a lot more time with their mothers than their sons, and as a result, they would look up to their mothers as role models.

The narcissistic mother will always think of her daughter as a threat and a subordinate extension to herself. She'll use the twin blades of criticism and control so she can mold her daughter into a more acceptable version, usually into the person she wishes she could become.

While doing this, she will also project a lot onto her daughter, including the terrible, unlovable things about herself. She will plan her coldness, self centeredness, and cruelty, among other things. It does not stop there. She will project her own mother's perceived shortcomings onto her daughter as well. You might even notice that the narcissistic mother has a preference for her male children. This doesn't mean you should envy the boys. To be sure, they go through their fair share of abuse from the narcissistic mother and is expected to provide the kind of support that they could not possibly provide as kids. This is known as emotional incest.

The relationship between the narcissistic mother and her daughter involves a lot of shame to establish control and force the daughter never to learn who her true self is. As a result of the guilt and inability to find her authentic voice, the daughter becomes very insecure, unable to trust her gut or her head. She also assumes responsibility for her mother's displeasure, thinking she must be broken in some way or doing things wrong. She has no idea that her mother will never find anything she says or does to be enough to warrant love or empathy. Sometimes, things get so dark that a narcissistic mother's daughter will feel as though she should not be in existence.

This comes from her mother regularly treating her like an unwanted burden, which she would rather have aborted when she had the chance.

While some narcissistic mothers will do their best to lie about abusing their daughter and go as far as they need to hide the signs, some don't even need to pretend since they're married to men who are too passive to shield their daughters from the abuse or may also take part in the damage. The daughter learns overtime not to bother protecting herself and not bother standing up for her rights. She grows accustomed to being and feeling defenseless, so much so that she does not even realize when others are mistreating her in her adult years.

The narcissistic mother teaches her daughter to feel ashamed all the time. She shows her to be ashamed of everything about herself. So, this daughter goes about feeling like she could never possibly be loved or accepted the way she truly is. She finds herself always having to choose between putting one more nail in the coffin where her authentic self lies or setting that true self free while damning herself to never receiving her mother's love. When she grows up, she finds herself in codependent relationships, continually feeling the strain of denying herself and making room for others while she shrinks into nothingness. Since her mother rejected her authentic self, she also rejects it.

As a result, the daughter of a narcissistic mother finds that she has this deep rooted shame that she just can't let go of. She feels ashamed that her authentic self could never be loved. How could it ever be? Her very own mother could not find it in herself to love her for who she truly is. She could not accept her daughter, so who else could see it in themselves to take her? No one thinks about the poor daughter.

Beyond just the shame, there's the anger, loathing, and resentment that the daughter feels towards her narcissistic mother. She can't quite explain why she feels this way. This adds to the feeling of guilt and shame that she carries around. The only reason she must hate her mother is that, as her mother has told her and showed her over and over, she is a terrible person. Her mother's harsh criticisms must have some truth to them, thinks the daughter. She grows up feeling less than, never good enough for good things or good people. She grows up thinking you must earn love and friendship. It can't possibly be freely given, in her eyes. As a result, she continually has to deal with abandonment issues in her grown-up relationships.

Narcissistic mothers might take a moment to care for their daughter's needs.

That's where the care ends. As the daughter of a narcissistic mother, you find that your emotional needs are not even acknowledged. There's no form of closeness between you and your mother. There's none of the tender care that a mother should provide her daughter. So, you end up always feeling like something is missing, though you cannot say what. You crave understanding and warmth from the woman who bore you, but you never get it.

What you'll find is that there is zero connection between you and your narc of a mother. You have no idea what you need emotionally or that your emotional needs are valid and should be tended to. You have no idea where to nurture yourself emotionally or give yourself the comfort you never got. You may seek out relationships and friendships with others to fill this hole on the inside, but more often than not, you find yourself facing the same thing you did with your mother over and over again.

Growing up with your mother, you found that she only ever cared about herself. She never gave a damn about what you needed, how you felt, or who you were as a person. She would do her best to control all these things for you so that your true desires were buried forever, unacknowledged not just by her but by you as well. There was only ever one way to exist for you, and it was your mother's. Such narcissistic mothers pay more attention to themselves, or at best their male children, but never to you, her daughter.

Your narcissistic mother would dictate how you should look and behave, not giving a fig about how you'd prefer to be. She would criticize you until you were left with no option other than to yield. She chooses your outfits, your food, your work, even your lovers. It's always under the guise of it all being "for your benefit." She would still undermine your decisions so that you learned never to trust your discernment.

A narcissistic mother's daughter will find herself in unfair and unreasonable competition with her mother regarding things like her own children's love or her husband's love. She'll do anything and everything to keep the spotlight on her, not you. She has got to be the prettiest, the kindest, most loving, and loved one. Not you. While she insists that your significant other is no good for you, the narcissistic mother will nevertheless throw herself at your boyfriend or girlfriend.

If she is going to remain number one in your life, then she sees it as her duty to undermine every single relationship of yours. I've just painted you a picture of the relationship between most daughters and their narcissistic mothers. It's not pretty at all, and the trauma of it all can leave you with some very nasty emotional and mental scars. I promise you that you can recover from it all. You can recover from the shame and rejection you deal with. It will take some time and a fair bit of effort, but you can. It means you will also be able to break up with codependency.

The road to healing involves a clear understanding that all the things your mother said to make you feel so ashamed of yourself are baseless and far from the truth.

How to Deal With a Narcissistic Mother?

Every single child of this world looks forward to their parents, especially their mother, for intense love, care, support, encouragement, and a lot more. It is essential for a child to get the feeling that his/her loved ones are seeing and hearing them while growing up. But, if a mother deprives her child of all such emotional protective blankets since a child's childhood, then that situation is extremely painful. It is the harsh reality of a person's life who has been brought up by a narcissistic mother. A mother who possesses narcissism is not able to provide her child the required validation as well as the attention they require for feeling emotionally secure and loved. Such disorders may have an immense impact on the child's behaviors, beliefs, self-esteem, etc. The impact is worse and more damaging in the case of daughters.

Growing Up With a Narcissistic Mother

Coping or growing up with a narcissistic mother is not similar to a pleasant walk in any park. Almost every individual possesses some narcissistic needs and traits but in a super healthy form. It is just self-worth or self-love. While in pathological form, narcissism involves an exhausting and constant need for attention and praise as well as a lack of sympathy, understanding, and appreciation for others. When an individual is raised by a narcissistic mother, then a belief gets stuck in her mind that 'I think that I'm not worthy enough to be liked by others.' Gradually, the kids start learning the ways of fitting into those molds created by their mother for them. This, in turn, leads a child towards anxiety. She may also push aside her own personality just to please her narcissistic mom.

The mother makes sure that her kids always stick to her agenda for leading a stable life. If in case they try to assert their own thoughts or feelings, then their mother begins to create problems by including punishment, tears, anger, etc. By experiencing all such situations, the child slowly understands that their thoughts and feelings are not essential, inconsequential, and invalid. Such a child will suppress her personal feelings just for maintaining peace at her home. They often appear to be directionless and lost as well as face difficulty in acting on and understanding their own beliefs and values. Thus, when a daughter grows up with a mother who has this severe personality disorder, she is definitely about to face a lot of difficulties in the future.

Insensitive Parenting

Giving birth to a child, making them understand or teach the difference between right and wrong, providing them all sorts of skills that are required for leading a happy and stable life, etc., make parenting very challenging and, at the same time, a sensitive job. But, in the case of insensitive parenting, the child is the only person who suffers the most. Neglectful or uninvolved parenting involves a deficiency of sufficient responsiveness to the needs of a child. A narcissistic mother proves to be insensitive in matters of parenting her children by having inadequate emotional attachment with them. It does not mean that she won't provide the basic necessities of life, including food, shelter, clothing, etc. Apart from providing all such necessities, many other things do exist which a mother must take care of for the better life of her child. But, a narcissist prefers staying uninvolved in the child's life. Insensitive parenting involves either excessive or no supervision as well as exhibits very little love, affection, and warmth towards the child.

In some cases, the mother limits all sorts of positive interactions with her children just because she is too devastated by her own problems. Attending parent-teacher meetings and other school events is a part of sensible parenting. By doing so, one can keep track of the progress of her child as well as the child gets a feeling that his/her mother is attentive towards them. But, narcissists show their insensitivity by skipping those events and giving importance to their own tasks. Many individuals are also present who are busy setting rules for their kids and possess high expectations that they have to take every single step according to those rules.

A narcissist mother is never ready to accept her daughter's point of view and is also not ready to admit that her own opinion may not be perfect in all situations. Sensitive parenting means that the parents must possess an open mind and try to understand the opinions and thoughts of their child, instead of forcing a child to follow their opinions in all circumstances. In this way, the daughter may get hurt as well as feel that her mother is not giving any importance to her thoughts and decisions. In most cases, the mother does not even apologize even after noticing that her thought process is incorrect. The reason behind this is that she always gives preference to her needs and opinions. Mothers with this serious disorder demand complete obedience from their daughter and also want that their daughter will admire only her and nobody else.

Growing up with such a person becomes more difficult when she starts uttering derogatory and hurtful things if her child disobeys her. Using words that hurt the sentiment of a child is nothing other than a sign of insensitive parenting. A daughter of such a mother may from her childhood hold a negative feeling that she is somehow incapable of not doing anything and treat herself as a worthless person. It is because a narcissist mother often compares her daughter with other siblings or children and that too unfavorably. Such a person is not able to support or accept her child's needs as her requirements are always more pressing, bigger, and more essential to her. Moreover, a narcissistic mother expects too much from their daughter, and this, in turn, breaks the spirit and forces them to doubt their self- sufficiency. If by chance, they are unable to fulfill her expectations or defy her openly, then she will start utilizing emotionally abusive strategies for punishing them or putting them back in line.

As insensitive parenting of a mother who possesses such a serious disorder may induce narcissism in her daughter, too, thus the latter may start feeling that she is somehow superior to all other people. Gradually, even they may start believing that they are worthy of privileges and thus crave continuous admiration from everyone around. Indifferent and unresponsive parenting also increases the chances of developing traits of narcissism within the children. Moreover, the risk of developing depression and anxiety also increases when a mother is not able to control her own emotions and give unwanted importance to herself. Stress and anxiety are serious outcomes that almost all offspring face because of inadequate support from their family, especially parents. Uninvolved or insensitive parenting also enhances the chances of an individual to exhibit misconduct or various kinds of faults during the adolescence period. Such a person tends to possess a fear that she may become dependent on others, and this happens just because her narcissistic parent never allows her to make independent decisions.

People who are the victims of uninvolved parenting have a tendency to show deficits in attachment, cognition, social skills, and emotional skills. Due to deficiency of love, support, and emotional responsiveness from insensitive mothers, kids raised by them may face difficulties in forming attachments in their future life. Children of insensitive or uninvolved parents, especially mothers, tend to misbehave in educational institutions and any social events as they experience inappropriate behaviors from their childhood.

Excessive Praise or Pampering

Over praising may seem to be innocent at times, but the fact is that it has many unfavorable deep-rooted and, at times, everlasting effects on the child. One of the most common mistakes, or you may say the most common signs of a narcissistic mother, is pampering their kids unnecessarily to showcase their love. Pampering develops weakness as children start believing that every single person has to do everything only for them.

A common fact is that almost every single parent in this entire world is proud of their offspring's achievements or talents. Praising your child at times when he/she puts real effort into achieving something is also absolutely fine. But, when a narcissistic parent overpraises their child for talents or looks and not for his/her effort, then it will definitely over inflate the ego of that child.

False or over build-ups insist a child feels that she has to be excellent for being acceptable. They also never feel good about themselves as the excessive praise received by them feels unrealistic and empty. The feeling of inadequacy arises because of too much praising and this, in turn, makes a child get the feeling of uncertainty about her true abilities.

If an individual praises her daughter too much for her intelligence or some sort of talent or ability, then it becomes harder for the child to handle her life in future days. By doing so, the child may start feeling afraid to face any kind of difficult situations as well as a tendency of collapsing or failing grows within them in case of setbacks. Excessive praise of narcissistic mothers may also generate bad feelings within their offspring as they start feeling sorry for themselves. They also think that their mother is being manipulative by pampering them even when not required to do so. Unnecessary praising also sends a message to the kids that they are not truly understood by their parents. Overvaluing a child leads him/her towards being narcissistic in the future.

It is very much essential for letting your child get the liberty of being flawed. They must also know that it is absolutely okay if they are imperfect. Instead of excessive praising, it is always good to make the kids understand that there exists no such individual in this entire world who is completely perfect, and others would love them even with their flaws. Narcissistic mothers have a tendency to create an unreal picture of perfection. Such a mother believes that her child is absolutely perfect and that they can never do anything wrong and thus pampers him/her. Gradually, the kid grows up by seeing himself/herself as perfect as well as begins leading a life in such a manner. Not only do they love to portray themselves as perfect, but they also desire that other people must see them as perfect continuously. For that, they lead an unreal life by molding themselves into someone that they are not. In this way, traits of narcissism enter within the kids, especially daughters who are brought up by narcissistic mothers. They can go to any extent to preserve their perfect image in front of the world. By chance, if things start going wrong, then they won't be able to tackle it, and it may also force them to take their own life.

Excessive praise and love of a narcissistic mother prevent their child from cultivating moral sense. A point of time may come when their ability to empathize and feel the pain of other people gets killed. They may also possess poor social skills. They won't feel guilty after doing any wrong deeds or feel happy at the success of their friends or siblings. Narcissistic mothers are unable to help the kids in building up their self-confidence just because of unwanted or overpraising. The kids start possessing a belief that they are superior to others and are thus not capable of making their own decisions.

Excessive Criticism

Another sign of mothers having a narcissistic personality disorder is that they have an expectation of being constantly admired and are unable to face as well as react badly even to the slightest form of criticism or disagreements. They look at criticism as a personal attack as the ability to take criticism sportingly depends on how secure they feel about themselves. People with narcissistic tendencies or NPD are just unable to digest any sort of criticism. Thus, they even possess a tendency to criticize their offspring quickly, no matter what the situation is. Such people have the habit of turning the entire blame to other people, especially their female child. Excessive blame or criticism weakens a child's self-esteem. Slight criticism, or you may say constructive criticism with a good intention, is required for a child's improvement so that he/she is able to become successful in the competitive world. But, mothers who have this serious disorder often feel that they have the right as well as the responsibility to criticize their daughters every now and then.

Due to repeated criticism from a mother, certain characteristics such as hatred, anger, and disobedience build in a child's mind. If a mother criticizes her offspring in almost all matters- be it minor or major, then a feeling grows within their mind that their mom has no affection and love for them. They even start feeling that they are unworthy of almost everything and are incapable of doing even simple tasks. Gradually, they will stop taking any sort of initiative both in their personal and professional lives. Excessive criticism is one of the worst as well as the most common mistakes of parenting by narcissistic mothers, which affect the kids very badly and is highly damaging for building their character in the future days. It even undermines the feeling of purpose and self-confidence of the affected children. Moreover, various types of unhealthy attitudes start developing in their minds. Persistent and extreme criticism is deeply destructive as it destroys the relationship of the mother with her children. The child will slowly stop themselves from giving any positive effort to rebuild or strengthen the bonding with their mother. The reason behind this is that they feel their mother will criticize them for such efforts, too, and thus the distance between them starts becoming wider.

The more frequently this destructive cycle of criticism repeats itself, the more damage it will cause to the family bonding as well as the child. They get a feeling that they are getting trapped in the harmful cycle of excessive criticism, and for that, they withdraw themselves more from their caretakers as well as push back angrily. Instead of exerting beneficial influence, too much criticism of a narcissistic mother demoralizes the daughters a lot. Various authentic researches have stated that mothers who exhibit unneccessary strictness and for maintaining that strict attitude criticizes their children from the morning till night, usually produce individuals possessing extremely low self-esteem.

The behavior of such children is also poorer than the kids who experience less criticism and are not so frequently controlled by their parents. By receiving extreme disapproval and judgment on a continuous basis, the female child of a narcissistic mother becomes incapable of internalizing the responsibility and self-discipline required for thriving as an adult. They begin to have a look at the directions said or shown by their mothers because they stop trusting in their own abilities to guide their personal lives. They even move away from those relationships and activities that have a connection with their self-esteem. Moreover, such individuals engage themselves in behaviors that are both self-destructive and self-defeating in nature.

Trauma

According to numerous trust-worthy researches, individuals who are raised in or brought up by a narcissistic mother will possess a record of facing complex trauma. Almost all children learn from a mother with NPD that this entire world is absolutely unreliable. The abusive and non-caring nature of such mothers forces their kids to believe that they must not expect others to meet their needs; instead, they have to fulfill the needs of others for being loved. But, the truth is that it is not loving and is simply exploitation. The early lessons that a person learns in his/her childhood days related to relationships cannot be unlearned so easily even after reaching adulthood.

A female child raised by a narcissistic mother feels scared of expressing her personal emotions. The reason behind this is that they experience no space for acknowledgment, affection, or validation in their childhood. Their mothers express anger and possess a controlling and demanding nature. Moreover, some are there who use their kids for serving their own purposes as well as give punishment if their offspring become bold enough or rather show a daring nature for expressing their personal needs. Those kids even face difficulty in setting their own limits or knowing their own boundaries. Getting punished for expressing their personal needs gradually turns out to be a trauma for them. They are unable to come out of this trauma and thus become excessively tolerant. Their tolerance reaches such an extent that they never ask any questions to anyone as well as permit other people to treat or exploit them badly.

Such trauma is very much destructive for daughters of those mothers having narcissism. They become silent victims from their young age as they grow up within a suffocating atmosphere of manipulation, control, and power. They will come across certain symptoms of trauma like emotional flashbacks, hyper-vigilance and will have issues regarding self-definition and identity. This type of childhood trauma gets fixed in their brain and alters their ability to respond to stress as well as having healthy relationships.

Extremely High Expectations

In this world, almost all parents expect to see their child succeed in all sectors of life. Even narcissistic mothers possess the same desire. But, in their case, they themselves set high expectations not for their child's benefit but for fulfilling their own dreams and selfish needs. Instead of valuing and nurturing their own goals, emotions, and thoughts, the individuality of the child diminishes as they become an extension of their mother's personal desires.

'You are getting so much opportunity for becoming a gynecologist, which I never had. So, I want you to fulfill my wish, and only then you may do anything as per your wish. Until then, do just as I say!' – It is just a small example of a narcissistic mother's extremely high expectations from her daughter. Maybe her child is good in music or dance and wishes to pursue higher studies related to those subjects or wishes to be an interior or fashion designer.

Mothers having NPD are not at all interested in knowing the desires and needs of their daughters. They are busy dominating or forcing their child to fulfill their wishes. They want their daughters to survive in their shadow as they possess unreasonable expectations. In such relationships, the mother rarely loves or cares for her daughter if the latter tries to be herself by giving importance to her own dreams. Individuals having narcissistic traits are never willing to change their thoughts as they think themselves to be perfect, and thus there is no question of changing anything. Many-a-times, unrealistic high expectations of a mother spoil the passion, dream, or career of a child.

Gene Abnormality

Many types of research are being carried out to come up to a conclusion that whether there is any genetic baggage involved in inheriting narcissism from a narcissistic mother or is it just the outcome of traumatizing as well as abusive upbringing. When individuals grow up in the same family, in a similar emotional environment, and are brought up by the same narcissistic mother, then a sibling may become a malignant narcissistic, whereas others may grow up to be perfectly 'normal.'

No such evidence exists that a narcissistic individual takes birth with a tendency to develop narcissistic defenses. It gets triggered by trauma or abuse during infancy or early adolescence. Mostly, the traits of NPD are developed usually by nurturing. NPS is actually a disordered personality, and thus a lot of eminent personalities in the field of genetics do not completely attribute this personality development to genes. When a person is born, they are actually the sum or total of their genes and their exhibition. The brain is that place where both mental health as well as its disorders reside. Again, the truth is that a single gene is not responsible for any trait or behavior. A group or cluster of coordinated genes is necessary for explaining even the microscopic human phenomenon.

Protect Yourself From Gaslighting

Usually, an individual takes a lot of time to understand that he/she is being gaslighted by their narcissistic mother. Gaslighting becomes uncontrolled in those families where the female guardian possesses characteristics of NPD. Here are a few ways to protect yourself from gaslighting.

Firstly, you may speak with any of your family members or a friend who will feel the situation that you are experiencing or have observed the gaslighting. The basic point is to find out some emotional support for helping you feel sane and validated. They may also offer you a worthy insight or assist you in viewing the other part of that story. It might seem to be therapeutic and useful, but you must not make it a habit of seeking validation from others. Trusting yourself is the best and true validation.

Confronting the gaslighter is ineffective and hopeless as it can backfire. If you try proving something to the person by whom you are being gaslighted, it is extremely frustrating. The reason behind this is that they will begin to lie confidently with absurd opinions. In such situations, the gaslighter may act confused and hurt as well as gain sympathy from others. The end result of open confrontation is the victory of the gaslighter. Thus, don't confront.

Another way is to pen down your traumatic experiences. By doing so, you will gain more confidence as well as ground yourself to your reality. The gaslighter will be powerless, at least against you, if you stay grounded in reality. Make notes, save texts or emails of the disturbing things that the gaslighter says or does to you. You may show such notes as evidence because chances are there that the gaslighter will deny. Such notes may also help you if any other toxic family members try destroying your credibility or character.

Outsmart the Narcissistic Double-Bind Strategy

You need to understand one fact that the world is filled up with double binds. Thus, it is highly essential to maintain your integrity. The misconception or illusion related to double bind occurs only when a person imagines that he/she is the only person who is responsible for all the results. You might get a feeling that you are not welcome. One of the best ways to outsmart the narcissistic double-bind strategy is by realizing that almost all individuals in this world are left with options. Another way of dealing with double binds smartly is by choosing to stay connected with people who prefer to respect your integrity.

To deal with narcissistic double binds, an individual needs to be true to himself/herself. If you are unable to be real to yourself, then truly speaking, there is nothing left that you may give to other people. Even if you try a lot to move along with your narcissistic mother, you can't. You may refer to it to be the natural rule of sowing and then reaping, but actually, life rewards every single action. Double binds arise when you need to choose between your life and the narcissist's life. But, you must always keep one thing in mind that by sacrificing your character for pleasing other people, you will simply sacrifice your personal happiness and peace. You must always speak out the truth, no matter to what extent your voice trembles or your relationship is threatened.

Move Out From the Toxic Environment

A narcissistic mother may turn your life to be miserable by being controlling, critical, and manipulative. But, you may move out of such a toxic environment by following certain steps. Firstly, you need to stop yourself from pleasing them. Almost everyone wishes for their mother to approve, but it is not possible to please toxic parents. You need to set as well as enforce boundaries because it assists in setting clear limits and expectations as to how others need to treat you. But, setting limits with narcissistic mothers is a bit difficult as they never respect boundaries. It is important for every single healthy relationship.

Another step is that you must not attempt to change such people as you will find it to be a complete waste of your valuable energy. Instead of that, you better focus on the things that are in your control, such as your behavior, choices, etc. You must always keep a simple exit strategy and utilize it when you observe that things are deteriorating. It is better to be careful about the things that you are sharing with our narcissistic mother. There is no obligation that you have to tell everything to your parents. Share only that much you feel safe and comfortable.

No Contact With the Narcissistic Mother

Yes, you are reading it right. 'No contact.' It refers to cutting off entire contact with the narcissistic mother. The truth is that it is actually a huge decision as it is quite a challenging task. Though it is an option, yet in most cases, no contact is the ultimate acceptable option. The basic step of keeping low or no contact is realizing that you can do it confidently. You have to give up your dream or desire of having a caring, empathetic mother. By stopping yourself from playing the ideal role of a good daughter, you will be able to control your own life. You have to understand that nothing is going to change until and unless you take the initiative.

Taking Back Your Power

Mothers having NPD have a tendency of observing their lives as monochrome: a world that only has winners and losers. They train their kids not to focus on their personal needs, instead give complete attention to their mother. But, you may take back your power as you grow up. An effective way is by seeing beyond the narcissistic facade. Individuals with NPD are pretenders, and they are scared of seeing themselves as ignorant, flawed as well as don't like feeling embarrassed or powerless. Once you are aware of their fears and behaviors, you must stop taking everything personally. You must stop wondering about your mistakes.

Another way is using your voice confidently. You must learn to confront and use humor when your narcissistic mother tries to put the blame on you. Your mom may have misbehaved when you asked questions, experimented, or communicated your views. But, you must not distrust yourself and regain your power and confidence. If you are brought up by a narcissistic mother, then there may be a lack of balance in your life. But, an excellent way to get back perfect balance is by doing just the opposite that your mother wants you to do.

Thus, you must not give any sort of emotion as a narcissistic individual will use it to manipulate you. Regain your power by being vague and stop yourself from arguing back as giving no response proves to be very powerful.

Mental Manipulation and Control

Control Manipulation refers to the use of indirect tactics to control specific behavior, relationship, and emotions. Manipulation is trying to get someone to do something that they don't want to do, making sure that they end up doing what you want.

Manipulation can be both positive and negative. You might manipulate someone to do what you want for the benefit of both of you or use to do something that isn't beneficial, only for your services.

In narcissistic relationships, manipulation has many consequences, and it is usually associated with a lot of emotional abuse, especially when you share a tight bond with the other person. Many people negatively look at manipulation, especially when it hurts the person's emotional and mental health that manipulates.

A Narcissist will manipulate you so that they are in total control of the environment and the surroundings you live in. The urge to drive you stems from the fact that they have a deep form of anxiety or fear that they can't work with. When you are the victim of manipulation, you will experience a wide range of effects.

Why Do Mothers Manipulate?

There are many reasons why a narcissistic mother chooses to manipulate the kids. The grounds will, however, vary from one person to the next. However, there are a few reasons why people end up using others, and these include:

· They feel worthless, helpless, and hopeless.

· They have the fear that their kids will abandon them.

· They have the innate need for control and power over other people.

· They have the willingness to use their feelings in front of the needs of others.

· The need to raise their self-esteem.

Signs of Manipulative Mothers

1. They Prey on Your Weaknesses

People that manipulate others have mastered deception to a very high level.

They will appear sincere and respectable in their dealings, but deep within them, it is just a facade. It is a way to draw you in to be in a relationship or do something for them before showing their true colors.

The manipulative mother isn't genuinely interested in you as a person rather than the vehicle that will allow her to gain control so that you become an object in their many games.

They have several ways that they do this; for instance, they will grab anything you say or do, then will twist it around so that it is not in any form recognizable to you. They will try to complicate issues and confuse you, even making it feel like you are the crazy one in any relationship.

They will change the truth around and will resort to lies if it serves their beliefs and helps them get their needs.

They will also try to be the victim when, in reality, you are the one affected.

The aim is to try and paint you in a gloomy picture so that they stay in the limelight. If they are the ones that caused a problem, they will not be there to take any responsibility for it; instead will prey on your fears and insecurities.

One of the techniques is to make you defensive. They threaten and bully you so that you can submit to their world of thought.

Here are the top traits of manipulative people; you can know what to watch when one comes along.

2. They Lack Insight

Manipulative mothers don't know how to engage with people, and to this end, they create specific scenarios that will absolve them of any responsibility. They believe that the only way to deal with the situation between them, you, or your husband is to ensure that their needs meet. It is all that matters in the relationship with other people.

All the situations and anything else is about what they will feel, what they want, and what other people think about them. What other people think doesn't matter at all.

They don't have the time to question themselves to know what the issue is; instead, they only see the problem to be someone else.

3. They Don't Give in to Boundaries

Manipulative mothers don't know what a boundary is. They will go after what they want without any regard to who gets hurt when they go for their goals. They will crowd your space in all ways without little or no concern over what you feel.

They don't know what you need in your space, and they will tell you that they don't care what you do or how you do it, as long as you give in to their needs.

When they are always in your space, they will end up weakening you, demeaning you, depleting your energy, and even making you fail.

4. Always Blaming Others

Manipulative mothers avoid any responsibilities that come their way by blaming others for causing the issue. They understand what manipulation is, but they don't see anything wrong with putting the burden on someone else.

They get satisfaction when you take up the responsibility that means to be theirs. I will try to use the obligation to satisfy needs and leave no room for you to fulfill yours.

5. Are Predators

A predator is someone that preys on your vulnerabilities at all times.

Manipulative mothers will prey on any weakness you have – emotional sensitivity and anything they can get a hold of that they know will make you bow to their orders.

They know that you have a kind heart, so they will use this to make you do what they want.

They might go after your kindness and goodness at first, praising you for the beautiful person that you are. But this is all about getting you into their web of deceit. Over time, the praises will reduce because they want to use you, then let you go. They don't care so much about you – what they care about is what you can do for them to make them happy.

6. They Talk Ill About Others

If you want to know the Manipulative mother's real intention, and then pay attention to how they talk about other people about what you do for them.

What they tell you about other people is what they will tell others about you.

They have mastered the art of "triangulation, whereby they come up with various scenarios and then create an environment of jealousy, rivalry and create many disharmonies.

7. They Invite You to their "Space."

One of the most significant signs of a master manipulator is that they find a way to get you to their space so that they can' take control of the situation.

The mother might have come up with a personal space that they feel they have total control of; this might be their bedroom or the kitchen.

The personal space for a manipulator is usually away from other people that might interfere in the process of manipulating you. Their comfort zone will make you feel like a stranger, even when it is a home that you have lived in for many years, and you won't be able to speak up against her.

8. They Pretend to Listen

At first, you will think that she is an excellent listener and see it as acceptable behavior, but what they are after is looking for loopholes in what you are saying so that they can discredit you.

They look for the holes to find something to criticize you and then judge you to fulfill their egos.

They will let you talk from start to finish all day and then turn around and use this information against you. They can even bring up any secret that you shared with them in front of other people.

9. They Exaggerate

Manipulative mothers will find a way to turn around the truth so that it works in their favor. Even when you realize that they have turned around the fact, they will brush it off in a ginger way and come up with hidden truths in the same words that you said.

They will take what you said and look for a few words that will make the same seem like a half-truth. If you decide to challenge them, they will twist the truth and negatively paint you.

To confuse you further, they will often use a lot of information to know how and when to respond. The aim is to make you feel so overwhelmed that you cannot process the information overload.

As a result, they end up deciding for you, and all you have to do to go along with what they say or do.

10. They Block You

It is prevalent when you are doing something with your mother at home. Let us say that you have gone to the supermarket to get a few items for dinner, and you arrive there, and whenever you request something, she blocks you. The aim isn't even about a lack of money, but she wants to show you that she is the one in control and you have nothing to do. She will give you so many roadblocks so that you are too frustrated to succumb to what the mother wants.

11. They Are Loud

For some reason, Manipulative mothers think that if they talk in a loud voice, they will sound smarter than anyone else in the room. They also always believe that talking louder makes them look smart in front of other people.

They do this all the time. Do you remember when you went to an event, and your mother was the loudest in the room till you became embarrassed?

The loudness is all about trying to push you into submission. You will never be successful if you engage in a shouting match with your narcissistic mother.

Even when you try to interject, they keep talking, with no regard for what you are trying to say. It will accompany the talks with a lot of aggressive body movements. They will speak louder so that they can gain control over everyone else in the room. You have no choice but to hear them out.

12. Always Negative

Manipulative mothers aren't happy people, and this reflects through both life and work. They will yell and scream at all people, regardless of their age and status. They might also decide to go silent, and in all this, they are enjoying immensely.

It is because they are unhappy that they want everyone else to share in their unhappiness. When other people are sick, they see that they are in full control of the situation, but what they do ruins everyone's environment.

13. They Have Conditions

They will give you a condition that you have to fulfill to get in their good books. If they give you a home task, they will order you to take it or leave it, please them because they know you are working under their orders.

They are good at what they do, and when they give orders, you won't know whether it is a bluff, or it isn't.

It might be very tricky, and when the manipulator is your mother, you won't realize that they are setting you up to fail.

How to Not Replicate the Narcissistic Pattern?

There can be a variety of different reasons why a family might become dysfunctional. A majority of times, it is seen that a parent might be a drug addict or an alcoholic. These kinds of dysfunctions are easy to spot. However, one of the most covert causes that are very difficult to spot is narcissism. Narcissism forms the very core of a narcissistic family. A family in which the focus is always on the needs of the parents and the children are simply expected to act in a way that fulfills those needs is referred to as a narcissistic family. Instead of fostering the healthy development of the children, a narcissistic family supports the whims of the parents.

The Narcissistic Family Setting

The parents in a healthy family are emotionally self-assured. Supported by a network of people, they live dynamic, balanced lives, and their choice to have kids comes naturally to them. As a result of this, they are properly equipped and ready to support and nurture the growth and development of their children until the time they gain a sense of individuality and are able to differentiate between things. The children in healthy families feel secure in their attachments and can grow up with high self-esteem since their parents are empathetic and have enough healthy shame. To establish order in their house, healthy parents rely on healthy communication and not on an authoritarian rule.

On the other hand, the parents in a narcissistic family live through a false narcissistic pretense and have long lost touch with their real self. For such kinds of parents, a family is like an entity and a symbol of status, which has to be at their disposal. Instead of providing a loving and nurturing environment for their child's growth and development, such a family becomes a well of narcissistic supply. The spouse and the children have to serve the narcissistic parent since their needs always outweigh the needs of the other members. Under the pretense of a loving family lies the narcissist's insatiable thirst for control. They enjoy their position of power. However, the other people around the narcissist need to follow a few guidelines for this structure to function.

Here are some of the unspoken rules that exist in narcissistic families:

Submission – No matter how destructive, cruel, arbitrary, or ignorant the dominant narcissist's authority might be, the other family members are expected to submit to it.

Acceptance is conditional – The children in a narcissistic family have to comply with the value system and narrative of their parents in order to gain their acceptance. Any expression of difference will be rejected and rebuked by narcissistic parents.

Vulnerability is dangerous – Any weaknesses, accidents, or mistakes can become a cause of shame for the narcissistic parents, and thus, the children might be treated badly because of it for years.

Blaming – When something bad takes place, for example, someone spilled a glass of milk or someone lost a job, narcissists will always find someone to blame for it. Generally, there is always a scapegoat in the family who is blamed for all the unhappiness, frustration, and difficulties the family has to go through. He or she also has to bear the burden of the dominant narcissist's projected self-loathing.

There's never enough respect and love – Love and respect are renewable resources in a healthy family. However, in narcissistic families, love and respect are limited to the narcissistic parent and sometimes to a favored child who they consider being worthy enough for their praise. Usually, they disrespect one person while respecting another.

Taking sides – A narcissistic family not only has shame and blame, but it also involves sides. The members are always made to choose sides. If you don't take the dominant narcissist's, then you are labeled as wrong. The children in such families are often forced to pick between family members, including their siblings and parents.

Competition – A narcissist family breeds betrayal and hostility and undermines trust. This is because competition, not cooperation, rules the day. A harshly competitive environment is created by constant comparison, favoritism, and one-upmanship.

Feelings are bad – According to the narcissistic members, it's selfish to have feelings that, in reality, make us human, protect us from harm, get our needs met, and help us connect. All these kinds of feelings must be repressed. Only the narcissistic family parent has the freedom to make demands, have emotional reactions, and express their feelings.

Rage is normalized – It is expected that the narcissist's violent, explosive, and irrational rage is to be endured and swallowed by all the other family members. Their behavior might also increase by other kinds of addiction and/or mental illnesses.

Appearances – It is important for a narcissistic family to keep up their appearances. They must smile for a family photo even if everyone else is suffering. For them, appearance is more important than substance.

No safety – No one is safe from the narcissist's rage and blame. Everyone is always on hyper-alert, even though a majority of the abuse is endured by the scapegoat.

Denial is rampant – All kinds of mistreatment, including the routine forms of neglect, the mistreatment received by the scapegoat on a daily basis, the continuous environment of fear, as well as the abusive incidents are denied to maintain the dominant narcissist's control over the others.

The narcissistic parent decides what role the other family members can play in order to improve the image of their grandiose self. They don't care about figuring out the best way to nurture and raise their kids. As a result of this, a sort of hierarchy is created within the family along with suppressing or shuffling of needs. This satisfies the narcissist's need for a dysfunctional balance. They will crush anything that threatens them or the balance they have created.

The narcissistic parent decides the role of each person on the basis of two things: what the family member can offer and the type of grandiose image the narcissist wants to portray. This image is generally portrayed as the following:

Image of a happy family – The narcissist needs to show an image of a happy family in order to boost their reputation in front of the public. This implies that they need their children to be extremely well-behaved all the time. The narcissistic parent will make no effort to fulfill the emotional requirements of their kids because they themselves are not in touch with their emotions. However, they want others to uphold this image at all times. They would never tolerate any kind of discontentment or bitterness.

Image of success – Success is extremely valuable to a narcissist. Therefore, the children of a narcissistic household are always expected to be successful in whatever they do. Even though narcissistic parents expect their children to succeed, they don't do anything to teach them and lead the way. The parents are only obsessed with maintaining their false image, and thus the children have to do everything on their own. This is an example of a covert narcissist family. In an overt narcissistic family, however, the parents lead the way. They want their kids to match their pace and exceed their expectations. If they achieve anything lower than 100-percent, they would be considered failures.

Your ability to serve the ideology of the narcissist determines whether you are going to receive approval and acceptance or not. The narcissist will measure you on the following:

How well you can sell the image – In a narcissistic family, you will receive points if you are able to represent your family in a good light in front of the public. You can reinforce the reputation of the family by showing that you are happy when you are in the presence of other people. This will help hide the misery of the family as well as the narcissist's real agenda.

The role you play – You will be valued by your narcissist parents only if you can play a role that satisfies the idealistic view of the family. Only then will you receive approval and acceptance from your parents. For instance, a family might consider education as the only way to gain success. Thus, you can get approval and acceptance by receiving high grades in school and college. Or, a family might value firstborn boys. So, you can automatically win points if you are born first and are a boy. One can also win points from the narcissist by simply not causing any inconvenience for the narcissist and being a well-behaved child. A child is often labeled a 'good girl' or a 'good boy' if he/she is being quiet and not stirring any trouble. Apart from these, in some families, being the youngest can also score you points.

If a child or member of a narcissistic family refuses or is unable to strengthen the ideologies of the family, they are going to be ridiculed, physically or verbally attacked, and ignored. A child only wants to receive love and acceptance from their parents. However, when they are only valued for some things and attacked or rebuked for others, a child can inculcate a lot of tension and anxiety within themselves.

Why Are Children the Perfect Target of Narcissism?

A child growing up in a narcissistic family has no idea what it takes to gain the love and acceptance of their parents. They are completely unaware that they are simply some pawns in their game or that their parents always have an ultimate narcissistic agenda behind everything. A child believes that everything is a matter of the heart. This is what makes children the perfect targets for narcissists because for narcissists; everything aims towards their narcissistic image.

Each member of a narcissistic family has a role to play. Some of the typical roles that form a part of the narcissistic family are:

Golden child – The narcissistic parent will choose a single child and mold that child to fit their own image perfectly. A majority of the time, it is usually the first-born or the eldest child; however, it can also be the second child. It depends on the agenda of the narcissist, his/her intelligence, ability, attractiveness, and talent as well. For instance, if the narcissist's image is the most valuable thing to them, but their eldest child is unattractive or awkward, he/she will not be chosen as the golden child. Instead, they give the title to the second-born child. The golden child is groomed as per the image the narcissist wants to portray, but he/she grows up thinking that they are special. The golden child starts believing that their siblings are not as good as they are, and they might even start bossing them around.

Enabler – One of the daughters or the spouse of a narcissistic family takes on the role of an enabler. The role of the enabler is to help put on a happy front in front of the public. He/she tends to the basic needs of the narcissist and even lies and makes excuses to help or please the narcissist. The enabler simply wants to be accepted by the narcissist and get their approval, and they can get it only if they act nice. They are expected to always stay by the narcissist's side and orbit them even if they are not actively helping the narcissist. By

doing so, they can help the narcissist to continue feeling grandiose and in control.

Scapegoat – The narcissists require someone on whom they can dump their disowned rage and frustration. They will designate someone as the problem child, and that person will be disciplined or put down at any chance. This title is generally designated to the most outspoken child or sometimes the second oldest child. The other members of the family might act the same way as the narcissist and end up putting their shame and rage on the scapegoat.

Surrogate parent – The narcissist will seldom care about what their children need as they are always preoccupied with themselves. In addition to that, the other parent might be busy playing the role of the enabler and catering to the demands of the narcissist. As a result, there's usually no one to care for the children. If a family has multiple children, the narcissist parent assigns one child as the 'surrogate parent.' The surrogate parent has to look after their younger siblings and cater to their needs. They will be held accountable for the behavior and well-being of the other children in the house. The surrogate parent, while trying to serve their purpose, end up suppressing their emotions. As a result, they grow up to be adults; they are often rigid and overly disciplined.

Mascot – The title of the mascot is usually assigned to the youngest member of the family. His/her role in the family is to mask the dysfunctions of the family by providing comedy relief. In other words, they are the joker of the family.

Lost child – The lost child is usually the most neglected member of a narcissistic family. They don't play the role of scapegoat, surrogate parent, or golden child and so are encouraged not to rock the boat. As they grow up into adults, they carry a burning feeling of inferiority or shame as well as a feeling of not knowing their true identity or how they fit into the world.

The role played by each family member can always change and vary. For instance, if the eldest child plays up or moves out, the role of the golden child might be given to the second eldest member. In addition to that, a child can also play more than one role. For instance, the role of the mascot can be played by the lost child, and the golden child can act as the surrogate parent.

If someone is an only child of the family, he/she is particularly prone to playing more than one role because they don't have any siblings. They will play different roles as per the needs of the narcissist. They are sometimes expected to play the role of a golden child, but they can also play the mascot to provide comedy relief and distract the parents, and they are also expected to play scapegoats.

Why Is Narcissism Often Inherited From Problematic Parents?

People suffering from narcissistic personality disorders tend to feel that they deserve special treatment as they are superior to others. They often fantasize about their personal successes and lash out aggressively or violently when they feel humiliated. Several researchers have studied and tried to find out whether narcissistic personality disorder (NPD) is a condition that is inherited from problematic parents. According to one study, parents who think that their kids deserve more than other kids since they are better and more special than others often pass on their views to their children. This leads to the creation of young narcissists who always think they are better than others.

A study named the "Origins of Narcissism" in children, published in the National Academy of Sciences, was the first study that looked at the origins of narcissism. According to Brad Bushman, a co-author of the paper, people are never born with a narcissistic personality disorder, and that there is a direct correlation between children who are narcissistic and parents who overvalue their children. In this study, two perspectives, psychoanalytic theory (proposing that lack of parental warmth leads to the cultivation of narcissism) and social learning theory (proposing that parental overvaluation leads to narcissism), were compared in children aged between seven to twelve years of age. It was believed that narcissism initially emerged in children in this age group. They conducted interviews every six months with 565 children along with their parents over a period of eighteen months. The subjects reported parental warmth, parental overvaluation, child self-esteem, and child narcissism. The researchers conducted 4-wave cross-lagged panel models.

The results confirmed that children acquired narcissism because of the lack of parental warmth as well as parental overvaluation.

According to researchers, the first signs of narcissistic tendencies can be found in kids around the age of eight. Around that time, they begin comparing themselves with others. The study asked children to rate their response to ten items every six months. They were required to rate statements like "Kids should follow me as I am a great example," and "I deserve something extra" on the Childhood Narcissism Scale from zero to three, where three meant "completely true" and zero meant "not true at all." On the other hand, the parents were required to rate statements like "It would be disappointing if my child was regular," and "I think my child deserves special treatment" on a Parental Overvaluation Scale. In addition to this, the parents also had to partake in a parental warmth test, and the children were asked to take a self-esteem test. The results of every six-month intervals were evaluated. They found that when parents overvalued their children, their narcissism increased. It was also seen that even though parental overvaluation was not linked to high self-esteem in kids, parental warmth was linked to high self-esteem. The study, thus, found that narcissism might be cultivated by early socialization experiences.

Here are some examples of how narcissism is inherited from problematic parents:

Narcissistic parental values – A child raised in a family in which one or both parents are exhibition narcissists who only reward high achievements and are extremely competitive often grow up with narcissistic personality disorders. The love in such households is always conditional. They will be showered with praise when they win an accolade but are going to be treated as a disappointment when they fail. Growing up in such families, the children don't feel stably loved. They can't seem to enjoy anything if it doesn't confer status. They only feel worthwhile and secure if they are recognized as the best and are successful. The overvaluation of success and status in their house and the conditional love sets in motion a pattern of narcissism.

The devaluing narcissistic parent – In a narcissistic family, the parents are very domineering and always put down their children at any time they want. They tend to have unrealistically high expectations and get easily irritated and angered. If the family has more than one child, the parents will praise one and demean the other. However, the one that was labeled as "good" can become "bad" equally fast when the other sibling is elevated. Everyone in the family is always trying to satisfy the narcissistic parent. The children grow up feeling inadequate, humiliated, and angry. They might grow up feeling furious at their parents and become malignant or toxic narcissists themselves.

The exhibitionist's admirer –Houses in which a parent is an exhibitionist narcissist, the children get attention and praise as long as they remain obedient. They are required to uncritically worship and admire their narcissistic parent's greatness. However, they should never even try to equal or exceed their parent's achievements. This method often results in the creation of closet or covert narcissists. These children learn that they will be valued only if they keep on supporting the exhibitionist parent's ego.

Consequences of Narcissistic Parenting on Both Parents and Sons

The brilliant post-Freudian psychoanalyst Christopher Bollas once wrote that a person's character is the trace of their relationships. According to him, people develop in context by obtaining parts of the relationships around them and unconsciously fixing them to their temperament, and thus, their personalities are born. So, what are the most common consequences narcissistic parenting has on children as well as parents? Here are some of the most common effects of narcissism:

Post-Traumatic Stress Disorder (PTSD) – In narcissistic families, one or both narcissistic parents can become abusive and traumatize their children and the other parent as well. As a result of this, they might develop PTSD and have a fearful approach to life. Since they have gone through abuse, they fall into a constant state of alertness and are always prepared to escape. This generally results in emotional numbing, sudden memories of abuse, and chronic anxiety. It can also cause a foreshortened sense of the future in which people are unable to think about their life beyond the present. To them, their future appears to be opaque and nebulous, and thus, they are unable to map out their steps.

Extreme narcissism – If a child living in a narcissistic house is aggressive by nature, they tend to respond to narcissistic parenting by trying to join in. They try to make sure that they are the smartest, prettiest, loudest person in a room in an attempt to make sure that others can't make them feel insignificant again. If a stubborn person is exposed to neglectful, abusive parenting since childhood, he/she is likely to become a narcissist when they grow up.

The parentified child – Children who are very empathetic, also known as temperamentally sensitive, tend to develop a need to fulfill their parent's and partner's requirements. They try to closely mind every whim and desire their parent or partner has. They are convinced that they need to prevent their parent's explosive behavior, bolster their self-esteem, and, thus, they organize their own lives around everything that makes the other person happy. As they grow up, they continuously worry about their own selfishness. In addition to that, they might also view their own needs as a burden to others and, as a result, hate them.

Need-panic – People in narcissistic households grow up to be terrified of their own needs. They tend to bury them by falling silent or becoming compulsive caretakers. They may feel that they don't need anything from their friends or family. However, if a crisis suddenly appears and they are extremely unsettled by it, they keep calling their friends and family in order to seek constant reassurance. They feel that they have to eliminate that need immediately. They become "needy" even though they themselves are afraid of their needs.

Insecure attachment – A secure attachment can be defined as the degree of dependence and comfort people have with others in a healthy manner. The emotional absence, abuse, and neglect of a narcissistic parent can make children in narcissistic households question how safe they can be in the hands of other people. Insecure attachment, on the other hand, can be divided into two types. The first type can be called anxious attachment, in which people chase after love and try to form the connection that they have always longed for. The other type is known as an anxious attachment, in which they shut people out in an attempt to manage their fears. A complex combination of consistency in attention, care, and the disposition of other people determine whether you will form an avoidant attachment or an avoidant attachment. However, unpredictable attention usually yields anxiety, and ongoing neglect can often create avoidance.

Echoism – Some narcissist parents tend to collapse in tears or explode without warning any time their children or partner tries to convey their needs or requirements. If the child has a particularly empathetic or sensitive nature, they feel as if it's selfish for them to have any expectations. As a result of this, the sensitive children are forced to shrink so that they don't take up much room. They struggle to develop their own voice. Because of this, it's frequently seen that they end up with partners who are extremely narcissistic.

Chronic self-blame – Even though narcissistic parents might not be openly abusive, a majority of times, they are emotionally tone-deaf. They don't really care about the pain others might be going through since they are always preoccupied with their own concerns. Emotionally sensitive children sacrifice their self-esteem and nurture some hope in their minds. They blame themselves for anything that is missing from their lives and start believing that they are the problem. They try to preserve a shred of hope by thinking that they will be loved if they "fix" themselves.

Unconscious Narcissism Between Parent and Child

When a parent's love develops into more of a love for themselves, how they wanted to become, what they wanted to become, how they believed they used to be as children, this leads to the development of an unconscious narcissistic relationship between the parent and child. Parents project what they consider as their "ideal self" onto their kids and try to create a "perfectionist and perfected" version of themselves. They make their children responsible for all their deepest desires and frustrations.

Professionals related to the field of parent-child relationships, thus, began exploring more about the unconscious narcissism between parents and their children. Parental unconscious narcissism comprises of the following elements:

Complementary identification of parents – The parent starts to think of their daughter or son as an extension of themselves. Depending on the parent, their child becomes a kind of an internal object to them to a greater or lesser extent. This means that the parents are extremely possessive of their child as they think that they are a part of themselves. As a result, the self-construction of the child is also hindered.

Projection of the parent on the child – In unconscious narcissism, parents tend to project the things that they feel they lacked as children, or certain characteristics they lost growing up, or something they wished they had as a child. They don't want their children to lack something that they desired or longed for and, thus, try to project themselves onto their child.

As a result of this projection, they get to see a perfect representation of their desired self in their children. It is highly possible that this projection could be unconscious or that the parents never really put much thought into their behavior.

Specific purpose – Someone with a narcissistic nature finds satisfaction when they are able to fulfill their goal of complementary identification and projection of themselves. However, this kind of parental behavior can also be caused by other purposes like the denial of loss.

A dynamic relationship – The roles that were assigned to them previously form the basis of their interactions with their children. Therefore, it will eventually exceed their imagination and shape how they form relationships with other people. As a result of this kind of relationship, a fictional personality is formed, which eventually becomes a reality.

However, children might react in various ways if we consider pathological cases. They might take on the roles that were assigned to them, and this could, in turn, result in certain disorders that affect them later on in life. It might also make them rebel when they feel abandoned because their relationship with their parents is limited or doesn't exist at all. The child can then start feeling that their desires were simply imposed on them by their parents and are not their own.

Separation and Healing

Separation from a Narcissistic Mother

If you're going to become your true self and whole at last, then you need to cut your narcissistic mother off. No, it's not dramatic. It's merely the truth.

You need to psychologically separate yourself from your mother if you're going to get to know yourself and understand your emotions. You can be on your own, without her. You can withstand whatever criticisms she has to throw at you. You can deal with the complaint you'll get from others for distancing yourself from your mother. When you give yourself time to get to know who you are, you'll find that you can be okay, whether or not you and your mother are in the same room.

No Contact

Having no contact doesn't mean it is temporary. It means leaving for good and not looking back, ever. Many people don't like the term no connection since it can easily be misconstrued as temporarily not communicating. The bad news is narcissists are like cancerous tumors. They have to be removed entirely and swiftly from our lives. If this tumor isn't removed quickly, it could spread or grow into different organs. There are times when we have to cut all ties forever. This no contact phase is like rehab for the victims of narcissistic abuse. You have to have complete isolation to cleanse yourself of the narcissistic energy.

Saying goodbye is having the ability to completely let go of this toxic individual without having second thoughts or guilt. You don't have to follow them on social media, be their friend, or check in on them. Severing all ties is the only way you can move forward after being in a relationship with a narcissist mother. Having a relationship with narcissistic mothers is an addiction that has been confused with love. When you are in rehab, you have to make sure you have complete isolation from all drugs to get back control of your life. It is essential to have a support system with family and friends.

If your insurance covers behavioral health, you need to make an appointment with a psychologist as quickly as possible after the relationship has ended.

Therapy will help you with self-esteem and find the reasons why you let them abuse you.

What to Expect When You Break Up with Your Mother

When you cut ties with your mother, it is very rarely the case that you will keep the relationships you have with the rest of your family. It's basically like you're a tumor, and you've had to excise yourself. She will make sure of it with her smear campaigns and the ultimatums she will issue to the rest of your family to choose aside.

It's not the final cure. Going no contact will allow you room to breathe, discover yourself as a person, heal, and grow. It won't stop your mother from smearing your name or trying to manipulate you from afar. It also won't cure the hurt inside. You need to work on recovery, and you could also use a mental health professional's services to help you get better for good.

You'll feel even worse. But only for a short time. It makes sense that you should feel relief instead, but that's not the case for most children of narcissistic mothers. There's the fear of being isolated and the fear that you've made a terrible mistake. You doubt yourself. Your mother has got her hooks in your head. Wait it out. The feeling will pass.

You need to work on recovery and healing. I cannot overemphasize how vital therapy is. It would help if you healed from the abuse from your mother and heal from the harmful coping mechanisms you taught yourself. You don't need those crutches anymore. A professional therapist can help you get rid of them for good, so you can finally soar.

Expect some blowback. You're free now, but that doesn't mean your mother is done with you. You might get lucky. Perhaps your mother decides to punish you by blanking you out of existence. In her mind, she thinks she's hurting you when she's only helping you.

You might feel alone and misunderstand. Don't be surprised when your closest friends or even your partner do not support you decide to go any contact.

All that guilt and shame. It's not unusual for you to second guess yourself after you go no contact, to wonder if your mother is right about you being overdramatic and sensitive. You might also ask yourself if you're doing the wrong thing, ignoring your obligations to your mother. You feel guilty and ashamed.

Feelings of loss. When you break up with your mother, you'll feel like you no longer belong to your family. You might be surprised by the intense feelings which come up. You might even find yourself trying to patch things up with your mother. As they deal with some daughters' loss, they also realize how much better their lives are.

You may go back to your vomit. It happens. You might suddenly want to see if things have changed with your mother. You may have forgotten why you cut her out. If you give in and go back and find she is still who she is, please forgive yourself and begin again.

Trying to handle an extreme and unhealthy narcissist mother isn't easy, whether you decide to stay in their lives or walk away.

If you decide to walk away and cut ties, the way you handle this move is essential to consider. If your narcissist mother isn't abusive, being considerate and empathetic will make sure you can leave feeling good about your decision. Just keep in mind that narcissist mothers can't empathize at times, and this is because of heightened sensitivity. If you can let them down smoothly without exposing or confronting them, this might be the best thing to keep their self-esteem from suffering a massive blow. If abuse is present in the relationship, you have to cut the ties quickly or safely that is expedient for you.

If Your Narcissist Mother Returns

Like any person involved in a relationship, your narcissist mother will probably try to contact you. They could be suspicious, angry, or hurt about why you aren't in their lives anymore, depending on them and the relationship. This is understandable.

If you decided to quit talking to your parents since their actions were damaging to your well-being, their parental love would not disappear.

Some people claim that narcissists don't love, but this isn't the case. They can't show or express their love in front of other people. Some narcissistic mothers find they have loving feelings emerge when they aren't around their narcissistic supply.

They could contact you in a rational manner that is caring, celebrating, or attempting to get you back or get something from you. Every situation, just like every individual, will be different. If possible, to respond to these attempted contacts, please remember to have empathy, but deliver it in a way that doesn't invite doubt, questions, or hope. Stand by what you know is best and be firm instead of being open to the things they might offer you.

If you left a relationship you had with an emotionally abusive narcissist, you might find they will get in touch with you in the future. It would help if you refused contact instead of trying to reason or discuss things with them. No good will ever come from these interactions, just more harm. If they continue to contact you and get angry, abusive, or emotional, not reacting might force them to gain control of themselves and move on.

If you have taken some distance from a family member who isn't abusive but has unhealthy narcissistic tendencies, you might receive an opportunity to have a conversation. This doesn't mean you will be opening yourself up for danger, but says you are trying to be present in their lives as long as they can behave themselves. If they still can't act, you might have to figure out if you want to increase distance or continue the relationship.

Believe in Your Power

Before anything else, you need to believe in the power you have; it is your choice to make, and this decision is not beyond you. Over the years, you may have been made to feel insignificant. You may also believe that you have no power to take the best steps of your life. Remember that this is not true, and the power lies inside you. Leaving the one you grew up with is never easy, but you can do it, so long as you believe in yourself.

The Right Time

The moment you have gotten a bit of clarity and started to feel your selfconfidence rising, you may want to take this step and let go of the relationship. But you need to know that leaving your narcissistic mother behind won't be an easy task, as there may be a lot of battles to win if you want to get your way.

Understand That Your Health Is Paramount

It is understandable for many children to remain even with the abuse being meted out to them by their narcissistic parents. Since they have been conditioned to place their narcissistic mother's desires and needs above theirs, it is usually hard to shake behavior.

Come to Terms That Your Narcissistic Mother Won't Make It Easy

Of course, your narcissistic mother won't respect your decision to leave. For many narcissist parents, children are possessions and extensions of them. To them, they are not meant to have any personal desires. Your narcissistic mother probably sees you the same way and would do everything in her power to ensure you don't leave.

Be Prepared to Fight Guilt

Throughout the entire process of cutting off your mother, you will have to battle with a lot of guilt. This means you need to be prepared if this is going to be a success. There is a massive chance that you may have learned to feel guilty for everything over the years, even when it is for your good. This is usually a way the narcissistic mother manipulates you into doing her bidding.

Overcoming Enmeshment

Know Your Rights

The most important rule when dealing with a person psychologically is to know their rights and recognize when they are violated. While not harming others, you have the right to defend yourself and your rights. If you break others, you lose access to these rights. The following are a few of our fundamental human rights:

- You have the right to be respected.

- You have the right to express your feelings, opinions, and wishes.

- You have the right to set your priorities.

- You have the right to say no without fault.

- You have the right to get what you pay for.

- You have the right to have different opinions from others.

- You have the right to take care of yourself and protect yourself from a physical, mental, or emotional threat.

- You have the right to create a happy and healthy life.

These fundamental human rights represent your limits. Society has many people who don't respect these rights; emotional manipulators especially deprive their victim's rights to control them and use them for their benefit.

You have the control to declare that you, and not the manipulator, are responsible for your life.

Keep Your Distance

One way you can easily spot a manipulator is to see if a person is acting differently in front of different people and different circumstances or social settings. While we all display a degree of this kind of social variation, some mental manipulators usually stay at the extremes, being very polite with one person and completely rude to others, or helpless in one moment and violently hostile the next if you notice that a person's behavior seems to change somewhat regularly. With no prompting, it is good to maintain sufficient distance from them and avoid communicating with them.

As I mentioned earlier, the causes of chronic manipulation are complex and profound. Remember that it is not your obligation to change them. You must focus on yourself and excel in your own life.

Avoid Personalization

Since the manipulator's job is to find and use the victim's weaknesses, it is clear that you might be made to feel relatively worthless or even blame yourself for not being able to satisfy the manipulator. In such situations, you must remember that you are not a problem; they are merely trying to make you feel bad, so you are more likely to give up your power and rights.

Review your relationship with the manipulator by asking yourself the following questions:

- Do they treat you with sincere respect?

- How reasonable are the expectations and requirements of this person?

- Is this relationship one-sided, or is it going both ways?

- Ultimately, does this relationship make me feel good?

Your answers to the questions mentioned above give you the necessary clues as to whether the "problem" in this relationship is you or not.

Concentrate on Them by Asking Questions

Unavoidably, psychological manipulators will make requests (they are not requests, but demands) from you. These "offers" usually will make you go out of your way to meet the manipulator's needs and desires. When you hear unjustified indications, it is sometimes useful to focus again on the manipulator, asking some test questions to see if you have sufficient self-awareness to understand the injustice of your scheme. For instance:

- Does that seem sensible to you?

- Does their expectation seem reasonable and fair to you?

- Do you have anything to say about this?

- Are they asking you or telling you?

- What will you get from this?

- Do they expect you to go through with the demand?

When you ask yourself these questions, you will see through the game that the manipulator is playing with you. You will see that all the other person wants to use you to get the results they want. The sooner you realize that they are exploiting you, the better.

Time Is Your Friend

Manipulators often expect an answer from you immediately to show their hold and control over you in the situation. (Salespeople call this "closing the deal.") At such times, rather than responding to manipulators' demands, leverage your time, and distance yourself from them. You can take back control in such a situation by simply saying, "I'll think about it."

Consider how authoritative these few words are from a customer to a salesperson, from a romantic prospect to an eager suitor, or from you to your manipulator. Take all the time that you need to evaluate the pros and cons of a situation, and consider whether you want to negotiate an arrangement that's suitable for you or if you're better off by saying, "No!"

Learn to Say, "NO!"

You need to say, "No!" if you don't want to find yourself in somewhat troublesome situations. It is not just about saying no, but you need to be able to say it diplomatically and authoritatively.

Saying, "No!" decisively is a part of effective communication. When told the right way, it lets you stand your ground without affecting your working relationship. Remember that your fundamental human rights include the right to do what you want without having to feel guilty about it. Learning to say no is one skill that will come in handy in all aspects of your life. If you don't know how to do this, then there is no time like the present to work on this skill.

Confront the Bully

A manipulator tends to become a bully when they physically or mentally intimidate or harm someone.

The most critical thing that you need to keep in mind about aggressors is that they always prey on those they perceive to be weaker than them. So, if you seem passive and compliant to the bully, then don't be surprised if you find that there's a bull's eye on your back. You effectively will be making yourself a target for the manipulator. Bullies back off as soon as they realize that their targets can stand up for themselves and have some spine.

This is true in schoolyards, as well as in domestic and office environments.

On an empathetic note, studies show that many bullies are victims of violence themselves. This in no way excuses their behavior, but it may help you consider the bully in a better light.

When confronting bullies, ensure to be in a position where you feel safe and have the ability to protect yourself. It could be standing your ground, having others support you, or maintaining a concrete witness of the bully's inappropriate behavior.

When a manipulator vows to violate your boundaries, it is time to deploy consequences. Identifying and asserting values is one of the most important skills you can use to "stand down" a manipulative person.

Conclusion

If you have reached this part of the book, it means that you have now learned how to identify narcissism in your mother and how not to give in to it. A child cannot thrive in an environment that is toxic and non-nurturing. But as daughters of narcissistic mothers, you had no other choice. However, it is never too late for healing. I understand that you might feel lost in life and have no sense of self, but all of this can be rectified with a little bit of effort.

I hope this book was able to teach you how to walk on the path of self-love and how to not be manipulated by a narcissistic mother. The moment you take the first step, you are already walking on the path to a better life – a life that will give you acceptance, love, and trust. This book is a part of your recovery process. The rest has to be done by you. Always remember that you are not alone in this – there are people who understand your trauma, and they are always there to support you through this. In case you feel overwhelmed, take a break – you deserve it. It is okay to think about your needs first. Remember that you need to have boundaries with everyone in your life. Healthy boundaries are the key to a happy life. Since you have taken up this challenge of getting out of the toxic cycle of narcissistic parenting, it's no cakewalk. But if you carry on with recovery, it is going to be one of the most rewarding things of your life.